THE VISIBLE

THE VISIBLE

poems

BRUCE BOND

Louisiana State University Press)(Baton Rouge

Published by Louisiana State University Press
Copyright © 2012 by Bruce Bond
All rights reserved
Manufactured in the United States of America
LSU Press Paperback Original
First printing

Designer: Michelle A. Neustrom
Typefaces: Didot, display; Whitman, text
Printer and binder: IBT Global

Library of Congress Cataloging-in-Publication Data

Bond, Bruce, 1954–
  The visible : poems / Bruce Bond.
      p. cm.
  ISBN 978-0-8071-4268-4 (pbk. : alk. paper) — ISBN 978-0-8071-4269-1 (pdf) — ISBN 978-0-8071-4270-7
(epub) — ISBN 978-0-8071-4271-4 (mobi)
  I. Title.
  PS3552.O5943V57 2012
  811'.54—dc22

                                                                                          2011030563

The author would like to thank the editors of the following journals in which versions of these poems first
appeared: *Agni:* "Choir"; *Blackbird:* "Hunger"; *Boulevard:* "Arcanum of the Other Leg"; *Columbia Poetry Review:*
"Black Iris"; *Crab Orchard Review:* "The Girl Who Feared the Wind," "Lamp," and "Milk"; *Denver Quarterly:*
"The Convalescence of Summer," "Lupus," and "Play"; *Epoch:* "Privacy"; *The Fiddlehead:* "New York Drive"; *The
Gettysburg Review:* "People"; *The Iowa Review:* "Day Moon"; *The Laurel Review:* "Constellation"; *Linebreak:* "My
Mother's Closet"; *The Ohio Review:* "The Strangeness of Knowing Well"; *Pleiades:* "Arrows"; *Prairie Schooner:*
"Zeno"; *Raritan:* "Ammonite"; *Rattle:* "Far"; *Smartish Pace:* "Elegy for the Lost Book"; *Southwest Review:*
"Empire of Light"; *The Southern Review:* "Blaze"; *TriQuarterly:* "Homage to the Left Hand" and "Ode to a Pair
of Spectacles"; *Volt:* "Underworld"; *Western Humanities Review:* "Memoirs of the Five Senses"; *Whiskey Island:*
"Homage to the Foot."

In addition "Blaze" was republished by *Battistrada Arts Review,* and "Black Iris" and "Arrows" were featured by
Verse Daily. "The Whiteness of the Cane" first appeared in *Two Weeks: A Digital Anthology of Contemporary Poetry*
(Linebreak, 2011).

For Nicki Cohen,
my north, my wife, my nocturnal iris

CONTENTS

IV.

I

EMPIRE OF LIGHT

After René Magritte

It's the lantern that we look to most,
there in the shape of a man with his dark hat
and radiant head, his arms cut short,
his face to the house that has no door,
or none we see, save the one the light
creates, as if the lamp were at the threshold
of its own design, however blind,
having walked this far in its sleep, alone.
It casts its blush against the closed eyes
of the shutters, against the gap between
their shades where the color warms
with the same soft fire we see in one
room still awake, in the distant corner
where someone lives or not, impossible
to tell, where some figment of our making
reads beneath a lamplight of her own.
The somnambulist knows what it is
to walk where it is neither day nor night
but both at once, as in the black tower
of these branches against the lullaby
blue of broad day, a sky-light that has no
answer in the mirror of the lake below.
The only fire there is the blurred coals
of window and lamp, the inverted
figure of our sleeper who lies face down
in the clash of ember against water.
To be both awake and asleep, is this
not one version of the afterlife,
trailed as we are by our own reflection,
to knock on the door that is no door,
and through the force of our own light, to enter.

BLAZE

God knows all that wrinkled in the fire
    that night my house burned down,
what it was I felt beneath the tower
    of light, there where it crowned
everything I owned or thought I owned.
    I recall the murmur
and awe of other kids who left their homes
    to see the brilliant flutter
of sky, as if it were God's sword returned
    to take back what He gave.
The moths of ash floated on the wind,
    and I thought of the blaze
of crematoriums, how my absent father
    managed as he blessed
his father's ashes that same day, somewhere
    in a chapel to the east.
I thought of how he must have held
    a book of prayer and lowered
his eyes like a child into a well
    where everything echoed.
I always dreamed the dead hover above
    our suffering like smoke,
that they watch the blunders of our lives,
    careful as they make
their notes, as if this were the last labor
    surviving life, the hell
and heaven of it, to join in the horror
    and tedium of angels.
Just like a boy to make a mythology
    of self, to take the fear
of burning and wear it as a name, to be
    that angel in the fire.
I never saw my father weep: whoever
    did, I'll always wonder.

Perhaps it was his gift to us, to never
      snuff the northern star.
Or his grief was some nocturnal cloud
      indistinguishable
from the dark around us. It's all a closed
      chapter now, a bell
without a clapper, a night without its sleep.
      What I do know is this:
once a boy stood in his PJ's in the street,
      breathing into his fist,
feeling old among the neighbor children,
      as if it were the same
with men, however strong, the way they mourn
      not with tears, it seems,
but with a nearly inconsolable stare,
      a sense of light from
the towers of their lives, their shadows flaring,
      breaking into flame.

THE GIRL WHO FEARED THE WIND

The trees know. And the leaves that flee them.
No root is deep enough to still their panic,

much less the girl who refuses to speak,
who breathes that much harder with the wind.

A mother's coat flares its woolen sail.
She kneels to ask, what is it, girl, why.

Some nights the girl listens to the branches,
how they scratch the sky in black chalk.

What is it to touch everything, being
nothing. Like the thing you almost think.

There's a questioning in the rise of weather,
so old now the words are worn away.

And over and over, the sigh that answers.
She watches a boy from her window,

running with his kite. He too is a wind,
a joy so quick he slips the thought of joy.

Not that no one holds her coat for her,
or coaxes her arm in the heavy sleeve.

But what does she see as her mother's
lips move, talking to no one. What does

she understand of unspeakable worry,
where like wind it begins, it ends. To see

a kite is to call a kite. It pulls her up
like the hand of some enormous child.

ODE TO A PAIR OF SPECTACLES

Folded on my desk, you stare
with the wide and empty eyes
of no one, just the impartial
gaze of the headless, no pupil,
no tunnel, no target, no bloom.
I am lost without you.

You the anonymous, and yet
the outline of the incognito.
I watch you float on the invisible
man, peering into the night
light of televisions, their eyes
fluttering against your lenses.

All those times I couldn't find you
to find you. Such crystal pools
I cannot pass my fingers through.
That is for the light, the world.
That is for the words you read,
the spy-cipher of the eye-chart.

You yourself are a language.
You take me far, or close to far.
And like a word, I rarely see
you when I'm seeing through.
What eye would be the moon
that turns to map its darker side.

To use you is to rarely know you
are there, save in the stray glint
that is a small fire in the corner.
In truth you are nothing without
fire, the kind that burns the bush
it never burns, or gilds the wing

in a Book of Hours. And as the smoke
of age takes me over, slowly, you grow
thicker, stronger, more extreme. Somewhere
in the distance, the flustered flags of oaks
and maples. Send help, they say,
their colors flaming, waving to be seen.

ZENO

The voice of the child you were,
will you know it when it answers
to your name. Will you cry out

in unison, even as the music
there keeps receding
into the hide and seek you call,

for want of a clearer word,
simpler, the way a line for instance
is simpler than a tree, though you

are calling from a tree, a height
the winter cut down years ago,
before your father and his frailty

were, like you, leaving you,
the child, something of the earth
he crossed, of the history left

inside his voice, his broken voice,
that dim day you both looked out
at the small waves, the approaching

tide over the tide's withdrawal
as if some sounds were quieter
than silence. Some distances arrive

without ceasing to be distance,
which is how you dream your future
arrives, though it never does,

that and the red-leaved childhood
street your father called to, falling
silent, or his part about the aunt

whose name escapes you—a second death,
you say, without the solitude
of dying, without the grief

you almost outlive, slowly, counting
footsteps he could not know, like all
things here you swear will never end.

THE VISIBLE

We are from the same root, you and I.
The tree as I see it is invisible
to you. And it gets more that way.

When I was small, I built a house
in the branches of an avocado
and raised my head above the leaves,

largely hidden from the world,
let alone the mother who called my name,
bewildered by my disappearance.

There is a tiny god in this picture,
somewhere in the distance. I admire
the way one thing leads to another,

how *to think* gives birth to the verb
to thank. Or is it the other way.
Every mother is a child of something.

Thanks to this, that, and on it goes
over the green scent of fruit
where it gathers, beyond the roofs,

the startled wires of the neighborhood.
Such a wide and ruined web.
It's gone now. The house, the tree,

the mother's voice. I am a boy
to grieve, I know, but some days still
the horizon circles all my history

like a bell. Thank you, earth.
I am a head afloat the heart-shaped leaves.
What I own is nothing to you.   .

NEW YORK DRIVE

After Lynne McDaniel

At the vanishing point on New York Drive
        two dots of light
approach us through the fog, two lamps afloat
        and burning, inside

what, we cannot see, save the drifts of white
        that swell the fire.
Too much light, we know, will blind a driver,
        one's own light

no less, let alone the beam a stranger sheds.
        Here it is wise
to hold back a little, to let the smoke rise
        as up ahead

you keep looking to the distant car,
        to all you can
and cannot see. There on the horizon
        the two dim stars

that tumbled out of heaven to the earth.
        They are the eyes
of some constellation, some quiet sky
        that laid its myth

beneath the shroud. You see in it a trace
        of something we
lose, or almost lose, this lane of trees,
        or almost trees,

half-eaten by the haze. And so darkness
        arrives again
though bloodless, bleached, broken into grains
        of phantom mist.

What is it that haunts the body of the world,
        as if we lived
beyond our life, here, now, on New York Drive.
        What we withhold

we let go slowly, returning as a call,
        to whom, it's hard
to say, to those in us who go unheard.
        We miss them still,

driving with a cautionary reverence,
        our shy cortege
a procession of one, lured from the edge
        of sleep in silence,

our windshield jeweled with a rain that falls
        out of nowhere.
Like us, it just emerges from the air,
        from the field

of weather, no cloud in particular,
        only a blur
that, to the laws of light, is every color,
        but to the painter

a lifting up, a coming forward, a scrim,
    a pallor, a hush,
a reassertion of the empty canvas.
    It *takes us in,*

as in *tricks, remembers, shelters, eats,*
    closes its gate
without a chirp. Across the powdered slate
    that is our street,

we make a tunnel of our being here,
    somewhere, lost
inside the night's remains, a stretch of coast,
    a thoroughfare

beside the moaning foghorns of the point.
    Look hard. Harder.
You are not alone, says the vapor
    as it parts.

The lamps you see beyond the rising veil
    close their eyes
in time. Day increases. Even the white
    begins to pale.

ORACLE

What it is we see we see ahead,
to lay the burden of the path we travel
over earth, each of us bewildered, led,
dawn to dawn, to part the living veil.
We worry, as mothers do, the world
steers as blindly about the child
as the child inside our traffic. The bells
of the courthouse tower tell us little
of the quiet shapes they settle into.
But we are a resourceful people.
Consider it a blessing, that part of you
you cannot see. Always a space to fill,
to sign your name as if it were a guest,
a day that breaks its silence in the distance.

II

AMMONITE

Whoever opened up the rock of you,
the auricle that spirals in your shell
less a shell now than a passage through
the vanishing point, a kind of stairwell

with its echo of shapes, its fetal curl,
that way it clutches at the eye inside.
Whoever broke that spell, the red crystal
that took your body over, that multiplied

where nothing would, and did, as if a void
sufficed to make a world, like a mother
lost in labor, or an old god who fades
into the solitude of prayer. *Whoever,*

we say, thinking of those who came to lift
your coffin door, to step the way a chill
steps down the spine, the chain that links a life,
a death. They must have known a child's

work, scratching at the dirt, as if to get
beyond the spacious boredom, the wonder even,
back to a place so like the womb and yet
more silent still, a mimicry of heaven

for those in black, gathered at the lip
of their underworld, christened children
of their losses, of a small past they grip
so tight it turns the future into stone.

UNDERWORLD

Last night a page from my childhood caught fire
and turned up to see if I was watching.
I too looked up crying *mother*, the way a star
looks up at the earth in the distance.

What do you say to the woman with ears full
of smoke and anguish, full of the story
she never wrote. Last night I tried to call
emergency though she was on the line.

Then the floor began to part, brightly, like a book.
Next day I went through my library
and thinned it. What do you say to the mother
who bends her spine into a question, she

who brings her child the *memento mori*
of a first word. And last. What comfort then.
What of the crack in the floor opening
like an eye to witness the death of all things,

even books. I always wanted to die
in a house, a book. I always loved the hearth
fire inside the books, even as they shed
their skins, horribly no less, turning up

to consume the house of my childhood.
There's comfort in the flesh, the earth,
the things that make us, molten at the core.
Comfort in the story that takes us in.

If only I could look through the body
like a page, to die another's death and live.
To be every story is to find yourself
in none. It's what suffering teaches. And fire,

fire too is a house. Some days a Buddhist
temple. Others a library reading itself.
But mostly, these nights, it's a mother's flesh,
she who grew so heavy with the world.

MY MOTHER'S CLOSET

After the burial, when we broke down
the estate into child's portions, to each
a broom, a ledger, the shuffle and design
of things we carried out onto the porch,

I opened what was once a closet full
of music, the vinyl now long displaced
by books, sixty or more, each a medical
companion, a difficult friend, page after page

flagged with the ragged slips of paper.
The stuff of faith, dire gospels, scores
of hymns with just one note, over and over,
just one note and a thousand horrors.

Doubtless they would argue in secret,
these pages soiled at the corners, the mind's
terrific passages shocked with highlight,
glossed with scratches in a mother's hand.

They made her the scholar of herself,
not of what she was, but of what she
could be, what she feared before the shelf
with its little study lamp, her body

glowing, lost to hours of waking sleep.
So dim, her books, she saw no end, only
the long dark well of questions, however deep
she bowed her head, anxious to believe.

LUPUS

Say pain is prayer in a wolf's language,
that's how Maria puts it, a night cry
worn smooth with use. Say it is a curse

raised up to no one, no God in the garden,
no hand to break the fist of the chrysalis,
to cup the flame hissing on its match.

Or the other notion: that pain is pain,
that what it begets is more pain. It is
the crimp of the badly hammered nail,

the body bent like an addict at her throne,
Narcissus drawn to the swallowing shine.
Narcissus, and yet a stranger in the water.

Wind or no wind a tremor in her eyes
like leaves. Who is this who walks on briars
to a door, a stair, a covey of pills,

the needle's prick and its small red star.
If only suffering had another room
to let, another story: a weathered coat,

a set of teeth, a skeleton to hang
its tattered flesh on. If only it broke down
in her arms, looking up as a man will

who can't quite remember his name.
Which is why these nights when sleep comes
just so close, pauses, turns away,

when the winter in the hour polishes
the slates of glass, you hear her in the distance,
tapping on the keyboard. Picture a cane

only lighter, faster. It's the letter she writes
to God knows what, to some future eyes
against the backs of her eyes. *Say pain*

is prayer, she starts, the crackle of words
like a fire beneath her cold white hands,
the quiet rain of sparks, ascending.

ELEGY FOR THE LOST BOOK

In Memory of Virgil Belew

What can I say about the lost book
you bow down to read and never will,
the one that chronicles a time so black

the stars go out, so tenuous the world
becomes another sky, another stand
of oaks consumed in clouds, so we are told,

the phantom shapes crashing to the ground
they mist. What can I say of the word
that never turns in some monastic hand,

that calls to mind no waking lamp or wound,
no cough we recognize, no eye refreshed
by a storm in the distance. What wind

pours over the wing, the page, the flesh
of the man we lay to rest, his body
a stitch of histories no one lived to finish.

I have known books that grew short as the day
grew long. In time they too disappear
blown from their perch along the driveway,

no longer standing open on a chair.
Doubtless there are books about the lost book.
There are windows that take us everywhere

we never go, that name the friend who looks
this way, eyes closed, who reads us reading him.
There's a heavy quietude that breaks

a code, far and yet not so far from home
we cease to visualize the journey back.
There's a vacancy that lights the room

that holds the book. Such solitary work:
the rip of the cloud in a lost man's eye.
At the length of our breath, a star of ink.

LAMP

We all look so deadly when we dream,
brimming with the other afterlife,

not unlike the grace the lamplight sheds
above the sill, how even in stillness

it continues to fall. Take the reader
who moves inside a motionless body.

She travels far into the smallest hours,
the solitude of the book in her hands

white and opened upward like an eye.
And afterward, if she descends, the fortune

of a cool bed that takes her in, to find
inside it the bitter, the child, the sky

of burning things. There is always room
in the unlit spaces, in the arms of a god

I talked of once, my back against a fire
in the woods, a cluster of sister stars

shivering in the distance. Nights like this
I am a book beneath the lamp of God,

though something leaves the word as I say it
like the wind that knocks you out of sleep.

Such rising to meet the kiss that wakes you.
Or the burst of anger that relieves

the man of his unbearable quiet.
How vast the world we would entrust to night:

the heart we bear with the broken lock,
the branch of prayer scratching at the sky.

Greater still what skies in turn entrust
to us. The sister star, the dead, the lamp—

all owe the dark their clarities, as if lost
in thought, in how the nearness of the night

is its invisibility, the smoke
in our jackets we carry to our beds.

CONSTELLATION

In Memory of George Bond

So many nights since your final night,
so many years between these words
and a motel breezeway in the desert,
overhead a body sketched against
the black, its eyes nailed with tiny fires.

It's there I took the aim of your arm
at a dead star in a parking lot of stars.
What stitches light to light is the same
strong thread that pulls them apart.
Their distance makes me smaller.

Once it seemed all my gods were dying.
Their very wounding gave them flesh.
In the belt of the Hunter, the ruby giant,
the sharpest, the closest to extinction,
the blood stone that jeweled the sword.

As you once said, there is no end
of the world's world. And then
you pointed to a space outside the lines
of any storied constellation.
You meant it as charity, though it scared me

to gaze at something as vast as nothing
at all. Who's to say my picture of you
is any less a mythy nothingness that speaks,
a drink to chase the bitter shadows,
the sky's spare change I give myself.

Still these days I cannot stop the great
collapse of stick men I lifted into place.
I cannot sleep save in the dust clouds
where evening's horses fall, stagger, sputter
like broken toys. Whose child are you now.

Do you go out as a gift made new
in the hands, if you can call them hands,
in the pinned eyes of someone else's gods—
I named them as a boy—of beasts,
of heroes, of the bewildered stranger.

THE CONVALESCENCE OF SUMMER

In Memory of Bert Meyers

Slowly the mouth of the wound closes.
The clock wipes its forehead.
Sunlight threads the eye of the steeple.
Everywhere you look,
a crossing over. The flower
torn open, a bending of the stem.
The bell trips over its own joy.
Welcome to the afterlife, it says.
And what could be better.
What we wouldn't give
for the cut of an earthly stream.
And it keeps cutting that way,
this thing that consoles us,
this intimation of going on
into a problem we cannot solve.
Birds whittle the air into slivers.
It lightens everything, their song,
leaving nothing. All light
is some small distant thing
that breaks. I want to believe that.
Just as I want the catacombs
of the hive to release their drones.
They are one animal now.
They are a thousand suns.
Sometimes the stranger thing is being alive.

III

MEMOIRS OF THE FIVE SENSES

They are the five fingers of a hand
that grips the world, or what we call the world,
laid here before the eye, before it welled
with light inside the tower of its well,
as if seeing crossed the dark threshold

between what we know and do not know.
Believing, we call it, however skeptical
its reputation, however soft the call
of day against the curtain's waterfall
we part to see the newly fallen snow.

The ear too takes, and in its taking tells
us something of our longing. All the time
we sleep, we hear it still: the tiny stem
of sound that descends the flower, the stream
that turns the chirping of the waterwheel.

Where there is a shell, there is an ocean,
a thing so vast we dare not call it a thing,
a great wave, or its buried lingering,
as if shells were just dead enough to sing
a whispered language of the word's erosion.

And what could be more quietly alive
than the nose, the throne of intuition,
our gateway to the labyrinth. It shuns
the foul, expands the violet, lifts a fin
of flesh to lead us downward in its dive.

Quick to rouse, impossible to master,
as the kitchens of the world around it
burn, or almost burn, or the black scent

of bacon waters the tongue. Heaven-bent,
it is the watchman of what tongues remember.

If the nose is the vesper bell above
the lip, then taste becomes the earth we're in.
It consecrates what the smell begins:
that writhing, that spit, that worm again
going nowhere in its teeth, its grove,

its little cemetery of nameless stones.
For some it takes a prayer to open up
the meal. For the few no holy cup
is pure enough. No mouth of theirs gapes
to melt away the wafer like a sin.

For the few it is better not to touch
the world, to awaken, body to body,
where the womb around us shares our blood.
We wear our skin as if it were a creed.
Feeling too is believing. However much

we grasp, however closely woven the will,
we can't be sure, haunted by the slits
between our fingers, by how a body lives
in the untouched dark, this place that lifts
our gods, the shining world outside the world.

THE WHITENESS OF THE CANE

When a man walks blind, you are the faith
he follows, the ghost pair of shoes, the beam
that sweeps the black fathoms of his path.
The time you keep steps just beyond him
there, no, there, the way a child steps
beyond the worry in a mother's look.
Or are you the mother, with fingertips
to read the world as if it were a book
of small sensations, a calligraphy of sparks
that welter to the touch. The sense you chalk
across the blackboard of the sidewalk,
it melts the instant that it leaves its mark.
Wherever you go, you tap a little shadow,
you rise, white against the white of day.

HOMAGE TO THE LEFT HAND

Not the south paw of the left-
handed, but you, the stepchild,
half-sister of the right, the one it
mirrors in a gesture of prayer.
To see you work another fugue,
so like a spider that weaves
note to note, fret to fret; to fathom
the great design of memory
and nerve, the body's music
that is your half of things, your
hemisphere, who is anyone
to call you the weaker hand.
Not that problems are any easier
being wordless, shoulder-deep
in the hole of the unknown.
What is it you hope to find there
in the soft light of intuition,
as your double takes the lead,
the pen, the rein, again and again
striking out to greet the world.
Ask the man who cups the curve
ball that slaps his catcher's mitt.
You make it the heart of the mitt.
That's your gift, your grace, your rhythm
in the most consuming tasks.
You who comfort the brother hand
when it is at a loss for hands,
or cinch the wing of the daily knot.
Ask the bride what hand she offers.
Your drawings may be innocent.
The name you write a child's name.
But without you where would he be,
the tightrope walker, his hands extended
like pans in the scales of Justice.

In one the dawn, the other dusk.
If you could dream, you'd be the Lord
of Dreams. And just like a dream
there is precision in you yet.
There are entire cities to build,
roofs to lay above our beds.
All night I hear you, silent, still,
beneath the thunder overhead.
You who balance the waiting nail.

THE STRANGENESS OF KNOWING WELL

In a world where anything can happen,
we're hardly surprised when anything does.
And so sleep is never so odd as another
morning. The radio clicks in your ear,
and the room wells up with human voices.
And who can resist it. The living coil
of the sheets you're in, their charmed tide.
You know the place. You keep arriving
with too many dawns to remember, and grow
afraid for the flesh that holds them,
for this room, this house, and so on.
It's the improbability of the same that haunts you,
the drip of the tap that walks in place,
same sizzle, same fly scavenging a blind.
Even the novelties of birds return to wake you,
what's left of you. Always your singular
body startled out of the dark like dice.

HUNGER

Take this phone face down in its cradle,
the woman there awakened by the bell
that never rings, that sleeps on the table
without the man who broke things off, who calls

back her marriages like abandoned farms
or some cold word her mother said. Take
that. Take all the little teeth she frames
in photos, the carpet she pulls in mistaken

hope to bare the beaten slab below.
Or the punished mirror in her trash bin.
Take the stars of every glass she throws
to fate. And so the hour she cannot burn

her hoard of letters but thinks instead of how,
yes, she will buy a dog, something to find
her here this side of the living, for now
there will be another mouth to feed.

And feed it she does: her bones, her hands,
the chest of every pounding door. With each bite,
each morsel of meat she dangles overhead,
there is always a leaping heart to snap it.

And while the dog bears the name of her ex,
she admits nothing, and in weeks to come
he doubles his size, his appetite, the flexing
of her bed, his cry for more blood, more crumbs,

more hide to chew, more squirrels to scatter
with his jaw. For what she does is never
enough to settle the matter, whatever matter
that is, never the thing to douse the fever,

though she cannot give him up, any more
than sacrifice the world they eat. She knows
that now, knows there are nights so mired
in stars and hunger she takes to heart, who's

to tell him *no, no.* And the whole yard stirs
to see her bent beneath the day's fatigue,
a broken gate beside them, her whispering
tenderly into his eyes: *bad dog, bad dog.*

PRIVACY

Forgive the older boy whose show of kindness
led me to his basement, who bent my knees
as if in prayer, the kind he used to bless

himself and things I could not speak of until
now, though I recall the thick white smell,
the musk, the mold, the salt. I taste it still,

longing for the words to take its place.
And yet I did not feel the full privacy
of shame until he held me to my silence,

which is to say I caught a glimpse of his,
how he suffered what obsession has
that cuts the actor from the act, his bliss

from my confusion. Even now surprise
looks back in the fear or guilt that froze
in him. What did I know of the difference.

Or why he turned on me, a sudden stranger,
and I an empty hall, a mirror's mirror,
and no less strange, this body now a mere

drug, a prick, a stem without the flower.
Whatever flattery I might have felt
crumbled, degenerate as a wall of flies.

Perhaps I hide my private parts away
by keeping my silence. And yet silence wakes
the sleeping man inside his sleep. It preys

on the child he is, the one who fades
into the flesh he hardly knows, his blind
compulsion red and rising. Like a blade.

ARCANUM OF THE OTHER LEG

After Oliver Sacks

What was it in the puzzled man who woke
    to the cruel joke—
or so he called it—as if some stranger laid
    a severed leg
in his bed, so thickly haired and cast away,
    its sour weight
insensible and cold, shored up from the depths
    that light forgets.
Naturally he worried who might miss it,
    what phantom mist
it trailed like smoke in a cloud of laughter,
    if ever after
there was something in his past he couldn't
    bear, or shouldn't,
some body he stepped on or over, a debt
    he carried to get
this far, or if the leg were some unspoken
    loss, no token
merely, but the literal embodiment,
    the *element*
of loss, a bedrock under the blocks of sky.
    Which is why
he kicked it to the floor, or tried, if only
    to find his body
falling there behind it, attached at the hitch
    where legs attach,
as if horror had found its one true home,
    under the loam
of his more vital parts, beneath their sweet
    and quiet meats,
so far below the heart on its summit—
    so hearts would have it—

farther still beneath the brain's starlight,
    night after night
its fire expelled from the world at hand,
    no end in mind,
      no place to stand.

HOMAGE TO THE FOOT

You with the intricate puzzle of your bones,
what do we know of your strands and hinges,
the arch that lifts the living tower, the trusted
heel whose very name we step all over.
Every toe a thumb, every thumb a pig.

And those nails that have no purpose save
to remind us of ancestral claws.
Any wonder certain corners of the world
bound or hid you, to domesticate
the animal there, the vaguely deformed,
mute, uncanny, inseparable, hard.

That's part of what he loves, the fetishist,
the thing we never place upon the table.
Or why the pedicurist makes you blush.
It was only when we cloaked you, worked you,
that you became such a ripening fish.

And like a fish, it felt good to release you.
The sprinter will tell you where speed begins,
how nestled in his blocks, teethed in cleats,
he lifts a brute explosion into prayer.

And yet aside from the kick of the thug
or child, you have no mean streak in you,
content to walk the rivers of our shadows.
Why is it then we blister you with progress,
or chasten you on the spikes of heels.

What once was last became the first to part
the fire, to test the footing of the minefield.
You live to serve, or so we would have it,
moving ever more slowly with the years.

Are you where we end or where we begin,
you who would teach us with every step
something of the earth we take for granted.
Are you not our children, you who wait
for pride to look down, to stumble, for all
those times you cry for us. We kneel to meet you.

IV

DAY MOON

Too late or too soon, none can say,
the lantern you hold out mere
rumor now, your desert Sea
of Tranquility nothing more

than dust, or less, dissolved at last
in the waters of the sun's rays.
You the dime that midnight lost
to the bright distance of a day,

the coin that rolled through a ruin
of stars, out the acropolis
of our dead gods. You the crown
that handed down its human place.

What is your vigilance if not
the scratched mirror of our light.
Constellations cast their net
in the morning sky. Too late,

says the sky, and yet too soon
to tell, to read your beaten riddle
of things to come, the afternoon
of those who walk each year a little

closer to the ground, who would pull
through the hole in you, the hole
of you, as if you were the portal,
the pupil, the wound that never heals.

A window to the sun that stares
at you there across the room,
you the Cyclops of the nightmare
sent to wander over the rim

of dawn, unconscious of a fever
daybreak brings. You who howled
in the throats of us believers.
We were children then who held

you in the evening of our eyes
the way a bowl of water holds
a drink, a face, a dark sunrise
worlds beneath the underworld.

PLAY

In my sleep there is no sleep: just me
inside a play. Not a large part, but one
with a little meat on it, with the style
of foolishness that puts you in black tights,
soft shoes, and a hat starred with a bell.
I wear my ridicule on the bus ride home,
too tired to care, I think, or know I care,
so when my body arrives, wordless, beat,
I feel heavy as a tomb in a bag of silk.

How the hell will I manage time, my skull
a costume room full of old productions.
And then the intruders: two men, two guns.
Who's to say what part of me is worthy,
why they batter the door I never lock.
So I point my pretend gun right back.
A joke. They know. I know. They wave the fingers
of their pistols as if some game were over.
But mine is better. I tell myself that.

For yours kills people, I say, and mine keeps
them alive. And even in the thick of it,
it all seems beyond belief. So what
does that make these guns. Just more props
to load, a chamber of blanks, a boy a girl
sketches in the dirt. Perhaps I should quit
this play. Such a crowded room I live in.
Such exits and entrances into the world
of work until even my sleep is work.

And God knows I need my sleep, a child's
sleep, full of the squirt guns that put tears
on the jester. Even the blindest sleep
is good, the outer space where the body

repairs itself, where the dead rise up
just before the curtain. Somewhere the scant
rain of first applause. The king is dead,
long live the king. What is a tear now
but a grain of salt, though real salt, mind you.

And what is sleep, real sleep, but the hose
we point at one another like guns inside
a summer day. Inside your crowded room,
a tiny door to the backstage dark.
The makeup bleeds flesh tones on your collar.
The heart quickens in the corpse. And rare nights
it's good to be dead, to be dead and alive
at the same time. To be somewhere between
the acts, between the salt of sleep and that

of work, between guns that don't work and those
that do, granted, as something to get us safely
through our story. It is good to be dead,
to be in the arms of the father who carries
his sleeping child from the playhouse to the car.
How large the oldest theaters of being
foolish, of the droopy silk and bell
on the long ride home, through hushed amusement,
the fade to black, deeper into the silent cheer.

ARROWS

Every thrill in us creates unease,
his father said, giving him permission
to risk the journey, to go a little farther.

But then, he asked himself, what of the woods
beyond the river that hold a cello in them.
Or the childhood yard made large in us.

Even morning asks, is there wilderness
that calms. If so, why. What is it exactly.
What in the sky that cools the land it stirs.

Or the brash magnolia that waves its silk,
that flags down the traffic of the wind.
Why feather the eye with flowered branches.

Is it not for the glow of the naked nerve
that the night bird opens the dark a moment,
or the painting shoots deep into the gaze

its arrows of green, as if want could be
a still thing, somewhere between the dead
and the living, the root and the wing.

PEOPLE

In the land of *People Magazine*, Tara Reid
    is having a hard day.
It's her body again: too fat, too thin, too much
    of a body to fit
into our imago of the prurient angel,
    perpetually young.

Here and there the combustible cameras go on
    and off like fireflies
that hover in the dark wood. You see them burn inside
    the startle of her gaze.
I want to say, get a life, but then it is me who is
    reading *People Magazine.*

So many aging starlets, so many bright white shores
    littered with the exiles
of heaven, with the desert palms and lemon trees
    that bend with ripened fruit.
I look up from the page, and it's my turn in the chair
    at the dentist's office,

my brain gone gray as the tooth I came with, the large one
    she scrapes like a skeptic
at a hieroglyphic. It's nothing, not yet,
    she says, only the seed
of the filling shining through. And then there's the root
    of another one, exposed,

the way Tara was that night her breast slipped
    out of her drunken joy,
drunken, yes, but joy. Were this the heart of April
    I might hardly notice
the cobalt blue of morning. Halleluiah, say
    the barren limbs that point

every way but down. Tara Reid, Tara Reid,
    chirp the dusty sparrows.
And who would shame the shameless of their joy. It makes us
    feel like gods again.
The deeper our indulgence the more we turn the smooth
    complexion of the pages.

Why pair the lives of stars until their bodies collide
    with insomnia and pills,
with all the bright white teeth of sexual revenge.
        The gods know a good
disaster when they see one, the kind that scandalizes
    a goddess, that roots her

to the common ground. So it is when the divine
    mingle with blood and boredom.
They too need a story to keep the cameras
    fluttering their eyes.
Another Tara sits at her dresser brushing
    a bee from the lip

of her wine. She suffers the silences of rooms
    inside of rooms, like us.
Another god's seed enters the human the way we
    in turn enter theaters,
the way the mind enters the hole at the end of a life.
    Only a dark like this

knows what it is to turn gray and fester, to bear
    the beam of hope we shed,
not far, but far enough. One story bleeds into
    another. Cut. A wrap.
And she exits the scene, taking with her a bottle
    of something disgraceful,

something we cannot see, no one does, not now,
        not ever. She opens
her mouth; we open. Some silences are so
        thick they touch everything
like the air that touches the objects in a room.
        Something kisses her lips.

She swallows; we swallow. And then she turns away
        taking with her the need
for some last privacy and exposure all
        at once. If not youth
then abandon. If not wisdom then mystery
        which is a kind of youth.

The common birds sing their December music.
        They sprinkle the sound like water
from the hand of a priest, in fear, in joy, or both
        at once—who are you
to know, they say, and no one answers, who are you,
        they sing and will not stop.

CHOIR

Once a year they let her sing,
the idiot child with the voice
of a heavenly ghost on fire,
too big for the body she's in,
too wild for the staves of this
one-room church, the common
meter of the psalm and hymn.
Not to mention the small pearl gate
of the human ear. Once a year
this bargain struck between mercy
and art, which is another kind
of mercy, which is another kind
of art, which spills its *alleluia*
over the lip of the double bar,
over all the others in the choir
until all music is her music
to relish and bedevil. Look
at the face she gives to others
discomfited with strange delight.
Look at how the phantom crosses
the chapel threshold of our pity
into something larger, more
rare, saying, *let there be harps*
to sour the wind that plays them,
let a motion sickness dizzy
the gifted, may you hear it rock
the infant to nightmare all
the colors of the sun, to pour
through the sleepy eyelids of amen
over the quiet that is not
sacred, and the quiet that is.

FAR

Whatever I am near, she reads,
you are nearer. Then she looks up,
a small boy and page in her lap,

each there at a reader's distance,
the sweet spot of the not too far.
This closet heart, the one that keeps

such dark, unreliable time—
is that where I am closest, locked,
in this thing I never see or hope to.

Or there, she says, *in this breath*
I take, this space that makes a word
a word, where if not here, where.

Perhaps this tongue, could it be
any closer than the mind
it slithers out of, or the word

in turn that slithers from the tongue.
Am I cloaked in the fog of streets
I walk, in the tooth I shine,

the glass I empty. Go away,
says the glass. *Away for now.*
Am I footprint after footprint,

the falling ribbon of attention.
Or here, she says, *am I the roof*
above my bed, the sound of rain

that falls where the rain leaves off.
And with that the boy yawns,
opening wide as the pages

close their eyes. He slips farther
from the mother's questions, it's true,
though deeper into the wilderness

of sleep, its ribbons and snakes.
A night rain begins to fall. *It's
raining,* she whispers over him,

as if the many drops were one thing,
their steady pour around the house
a house of rain. *Tell me,* she says,

*what is stranger than the sound
of your own voice, your own full name
you cut in two to name a child.*

BLACK IRIS

Dear guitar, my Cyclops, my raft,
my drunken bassinet, my doll
without arms, my willow, my ink,

what is it dies in the grain of you,
my hollow stare at the wall of stars,
my corner, my carrel, my final word,

what nights do you consume and why,
you with your permanent o of surprise,
why cricket, why thrush, why beg

with this bowl of tainted shadow,
this cold black moon burning in its box,
why now in my mother's illness

do I think of you as a gift
floating back from the end of things,
my insensible earth, my great felled spruce,

my anxious boy looking away,
why is she everywhere you are not,
why then are you her only name.

MILK

Ask any star, flame to flame, any infant
mouth that tugs the long and twisted rope
of light, that pulls a tether to the world.

We drink and so ignite the word for what
we drink, what consumes us in its music.
The mere mention is its own erasure.

And soon it arrives, this breakfast table,
these words we lay against our tongues like forks.
The pitcher tilts. The fire flashes as it braids.

We think *of* and *about,* and so the bridge
and the barrier of how we think,
the want that sets our thinking into motion.

When our mother tongue was just a child,
desire too fell from the night sky,
from the stars, says the book of tongues.

And since the brain was one enormous cloud
that came between us and the universe
we would conceive, one was never here there.

Stars looked down their rifles in the fog.
All we want would kill us, surely, our eyes
awash in the blood of the human heart.

And yet to want to be wanted, to flee
our skin like music from a radio,
it speaks of certain liberties, yours, mine.

Where there is power, there is no love.
I read that once. Can it also be true
how strong the solitude that overpowers

its own illusion, our breath repeating against
the shore. A surge peaks above the child
before it buckles beneath its weight, and gives.

To give, to relent, to wake each time
to a heart so quick you swear it isn't yours.
Which is to say you can, in some measure,

long for what you have, as if the trembling
of one body broke you into two.
Take the man who walks the streets at night

to remind himself, yes, he has arms, legs,
that he wants these things, that he moves
forever toward his lifetime in the distance.

Men like that talk to themselves. They wonder
aloud for the company of strangers,
unsure what it was that snipped the braid,

the face of sleep descending like an anchor.
Those who never dream are always dreaming.
The earth tilts. The clouds spill from north to south.

That sound you hear. Where would you put it.
Where to lay our heads like some luminous
breakfast at the end of our journey.

When, I ask, will the moment linger
long enough to share this meal, to talk
of the departed with a distant music

in its voice. Does it create suffering,
the light we drink to mend our suffering. I know
I talk to no one when I ask the dead.

Behind these leaves are holes the shapes of leaves.
I hear them crackle in the trees like milk.
Still I keep returning to my friends

swallowed up in that surge of fire.
Come out, night replies, and so the names
come spilling over in a trickle of jewels.

No star is one word I use for all the stars.
Come out, says the sky to the planet,
says friend to friend, mother to the dire

thirst that eyes the sister stars of nipples,
that puts its mouth to the future and so
draws the great white silk, as if to drain

the lamp that way, to dim the source that is
this cloud, this breast, this small ghost voice
as it darkly whispers, *there there, there there.*